G000071494

Presented to

Arrom & Donna

On the occasion of

_____

From

Arlene.

Date

_____

© 2000 by Barbour Publishing, Inc.

ISBN 1-57748-729-X

Unless otherwise noted, all Scripture quotations are taken from the King James Version of the Bible.

Scripture quotations from the Amplified New Testament are © 1954, 1958, 1987 by The Lockman Foundation. Used by permission.

The selection by Donna Lange is used with the author's permission.

Published by Barbour Publishing, Inc., P. O. Box 719, Uhrichsville, Ohio 44683
http://www.barbourbooks.com

 Member of the
Evangelical Christian
Publishers Association

Printed in China.

SOMETHING BORROWED
Something Blue

A CELEBRATION OF
YOUR WEDDING DAY

ELLYN SANNA

BARBOUR
PUBLISHING, INC.

Something Old. . .

On their wedding day, the bride and groom sew the seam that binds their two lives together into something new. But at the same time, their wedding also ties them to the fabric of the past, to the histories of their two families. That is why so many traditions are woven into the wedding day—like "something borrowed, something blue, something old, and something new." This old custom is carried out in many different ways. . .with a grandmother's wedding gown, a mother-in-law's blue handkerchief tucked up a bride's sleeve, a sister's borrowed veil. . .all different kinds of fabric pieced together into the day's smooth material, symbolizing all that the couple owes to the entire community and to those who have gone before them. Together, husband and wife will create something totally original, a brand-new family—but they will build on the old patterns, the legacy of love that is stitched into their hearts.

A Brand-New Tapestry of Love

*Y*our wedding will create something never seen before, for it will weave together the separate strands of your lives, fashioning from them an entirely new fabric. This brand-new tapestry of love will form the shelter for your lives as husband and wife. Beneath its pavilion, you can rejoice in total security, knowing that your love is not only beautiful and bright, but serviceable. So long as it is pitched on the solid rock of Christ, it will be strong enough to withstand the storms of life.

For in the time of trouble he shall hide me in his pavilion: in the secret of his tabernacle shall he hide me; he shall set me up upon a rock.

PSALM 27:5

To wed is to bring not only our worldly goods
but every potential capacity. . . .
In becoming one, these two create a new world
that had never existed before.

PAUL E. JOHNSON

*When you love someone,
all your saved-up wishes start coming out.*

ELIZABETH BOWEN

Love gives us in a moment what we can hardly attain
by effort after years of toil.

J. W. VON GOETHE (1749–1832)

Something New...

*O*n their wedding day, the bride and groom do not usually show up in dirty, old clothes. Instead, the groom wears a spotless tuxedo, and the bride is dressed in a new gown, a gown of white she has never worn before. This new, white clothing symbolizes purity.

The word *purity* comes from two word roots. One means "to clean" and the other means "fresh and green," like the new growing life of spring. So when the bride and groom face each other on their wedding day, clothed in newness and purity, they are symbolically cleaned of the past so that they can grow into the future.

The Greek word for purity also means "fire"—and by the power of Christ's grace, husband and wife come to each other in complete purity, a purity that burns the past's tattered, stained old rags, leaving the bride and groom dressed in new wedding clothes that can last a lifetime.

I will greatly rejoice in the LORD,
my soul shall be joyful in my God;
for he hath clothed me with the garments
of salvation, he hath covered me
with the robe of righteousness,
as a bridegroom decketh himself
with ornaments, and as a bride
adorneth herself with her jewels.

ISAIAH 61:10

Come live with me, and be my love,
And we will some new pleasures prove
Of golden sands, and crystal brooks,
With silken lines, and silver hooks.

JOHN DONNE (1573–1631)

Knitted Hearts

On your wedding day, you do not cease to be two separate people. Obviously, you will continue to be individuals, each with your own opinions and interests and tastes. Working out the differences between you will be part of your marriage's challenge.

But despite this, in a very real way, your wedding day begins the lifelong process of knitting your two hearts together. From now on, what touches one of you cannot help but touch the other as well. You no longer face the world alone.

Like two different shades of yarn that have been knit into a single garment, husband and wife share one life. Her joy is his joy, and his sorrow is her sorrow. And as their lives go by, with God's help, their lives and hearts will become one, just as Christ is one with the Father, and we are one with Him.

Be of the same mind one toward another.

ROMANS 12:16

Thou, Father, art in me, and I in thee,
that they also may be one in us: that the world
may believe that thou hast sent me.

JOHN 17:21

Knit your hearts with an unslipping knot.
WILLIAM SHAKESPEARE (1564–1616)

No cord or cable can draw so forcibly,
or bind so fast,
as love can do with a single thread.

ROBERT BURTON (1577–1640)

I think you are good, gifted, lovely: a fervent, a solemn passion
is conceived in my heart; it leans to you. . .and,
kindling in pure, powerful flame, fuses you and me in one.
CHARLOTTE BRONTË

Chains do not hold a marriage together.
It is threads, hundreds of tiny threads, that sew people together.
SIMONE SIGNORET

*Love alone is capable of uniting living beings
in such a way as to complete and fulfill them,
for it alone takes them and joins them
by what is deepest in themselves.*

PIERRE TIELHARD DE CHARDIN

Love is. . .born with the pleasure of looking at each other,
it is fed with the necessity of seeing each other,
it is concluded with the impossibility of separation!
JOSÈ MARTÌ Y PERÉZ (1853–1895)

Something Borrowed. . .

When we are single, we tend to rely upon our own resources. We look out for our own interests, and we protect ourselves from hurt and injury. We guard against becoming too vulnerable to another. No matter how kind or nice we are, we usually think of ourselves as the center of our world, and we put up neat boundaries around that center.

But once we marry, we can no longer keep our comfortable spot at the center of the universe, for now we must consider another's interests as well as our own. Our old boundaries that once served us so well will be crossed by our spouses. Sometimes, the process is uncomfortable.

But husband and wife are rewarded for their efforts, for now they no longer have to depend totally on their own strength. Now, when they are tired or discouraged, when they are weak or losing faith, they can borrow strength from the other—and by the same token, they share their joy.

To love is to place our happiness
in the happiness of another.
GOTTFRIED WILHELM VON LEIBNIZ (1646–1716)

Love is, above all, the gift of oneself.

JEAN ANOUILH

The best proof of love is trust.
JOYCE BROTHERS

17

The only true gift is a portion of yourself.
RALPH WALDO EMERSON

In love, the paradox occurs that two beings

become one and yet remain two.

ERICH FROMM

The courage to share your feelings
is critical to sustaining a love relationship.
HAROLD H. BLOOMFIELD

Just for the
Two of You

On your wedding day, a portion of your new life's fabric will be shared with everyone. Because the two of you are married, you will enrich the larger community; as you open your home and hearts, your relationship will bring new warmth to those around you.

But another piece of your life together will belong only to the two of you. This is not merely your physical relationship; it goes beyond that, for the depth and intimacy of your union create the robes you wear alone with each other, private robes the public will never see. This clothing is as comfortable as flannel and as beautiful as lace; it is as durable as cotton and yet as delicate as silk. Take care of this intimate clothing; keep it clean and mended so that the passing years will only embroider its pattern with finer detail, leaving the basic lines the same as on your wedding day.

Love can be understood only "from the inside," as a language can be understood only by someone who speaks it, as a world can be understood only by someone who lives in it.

ROBERT C. SOLOMON

There is but one genuine love potion— consideration.

MENANDER (342–292 B.C.)

At home by the fire, whenever you look up, there I shall be— and whenever I look up, there will be you.

THOMAS HARDY

21

She is mine to have and to hold!
She has chosen between love and gold!
All the joys life can give
Shall be hers, while I live,
For she's mine to have and to hold.

WILL A. HEELAN

Peaceful Intimacy

My favorite part of our wedding day was not the moment when we knelt by the altar and prayed for God's blessing on our marriage. It wasn't when we turned around and faced the congregation, husband and wife at last, nor was it the reception when we were surrounded by all the people we love most. Each of these were wonderful times, moments of almost overwhelming joy. But for me, the best part of the entire day was when I took off my beautiful but hot lace dress, slipped my aching feet out of the high heels, put on soft, comfortable clothes, and drove away with my new husband. Alone at last, just the two of us. The wedding was wonderful—but even better was leaving all the noise and celebration behind so that we two could relax with each other. Driving away through the darkness, not saying anything, simply holding hands—that was my favorite moment of our wedding day.

"*My well-beloved is mine and I am his.*"
Love was their banqueting-house,
love was their wine, love was their ensign. . .
love was his apples, love was her comforts;
love made him see her, love made her seek him;
love made him wed her,
love made her follow him; . . .
Love bred our fellowship,
let love continue it, and
love shall increase it until death dissolve it.

JOHN WINTHROP (1588–1649) to his fiancée

The Fabric
of Eternity

On your wedding day, your two lives are sewn together in all sorts of different ways. There's the practical, physical level: From now on, the two of you will share not only a bed but a checkbook; you will give each other delight and pleasure—and you will contend with the way you each squeeze toothpaste and whether you prefer the toilet seat left up or down. On the emotional level, you will find comfort in each other's love and understanding, while you will also need to make adjustments for your emotional differences. But a wedding stitches the two of you together at an even deeper level, for spiritually, you are also joined. In God's eyes, your two lives have been united, and the fabric of your lives together will reach into eternity.

For this cause shall a man leave his father and mother,
and shall be joined unto his wife, and they two shall be one flesh.
EPHESIANS 5:31

*Not that we want to put off the body
(the clothing of the spirit),
but rather that we would be further clothed,
so that what is mortal. . .
may be swallowed up by life.
For the things that are visible are temporal
(brief and fleeting), but the things that are
invisible are deathless and everlasting.*

2 CORINTHIANS 5:4, 4:18, AMPLIFIED BIBLE

Love vanquishes time. To lovers, a moment can be eternity,
eternity can be the tick of a clock.

MARY PARISH

*Successful marriage is always a triangle:
a man, a woman, and God.*

CECIL MYERS

Where love reigns the very joy of heaven itself is felt.

HANNAH HURNARD

Make us of one heart and mind,
Courteous, merciful, and kind;
Lowly, meek in thought and word,
Ne'er by fretful passion stirred.

Free from anger, free from pride,
Let us thus in God abide;
All the depth of love express,
All the height of holiness.

CHARLES WESLEY

A Braid of Love

*Y*ou will find you cannot snip your married life into pieces, separating the physical, the emotional, and the spiritual from one another. No, the three aspects of your being are plaited together in your marriage, and you cannot unwind one from the other. And yet working these three strands into one smooth braid is not always easy. It takes discipline and courage, patience and forgiveness, and most of all an undying commitment to each other and to your marriage.

Sometimes it may seem impossible—but with God, nothing is impossible. Keep on twining the threads of your life together, and one day you will find you have reached all the way to heaven.

Whoso loves believes the impossible.
ELIZABETH BARRETT BROWNING

Nothing great was ever done without much enduring.
CATHERINE OF SIENA

To love is to receive a glimpse of heaven.
KAREN SUNDE

To believe in something not yet proved and to underwrite it with our lives; it is the only way we can leave the future open.
LILLIAN SMITH

A Covering of Joy

*I*f you think of your lives together as a quilt, then you will find that your marriage will be pieced together from many different fabrics, bright, shiny satins as well as rough, dark wools. But the quilt would not be complete without each piece—and together they form a covering that will warm you and bring you joy for the rest of your lives.

So on your wedding day, sew bright happy colors into your covering. Be glad and rejoice in your love—and know that God is rejoicing with you.

My heart is like a singing bird. . .
Because the birthday of my life
Is come, my love is come to me.
CHRISTINA ROSSETTI (1830–1894)

*To love is. . .
what makes this world a garden.*
ROBERT LOUIS STEVENSON (1850–1894)

The fabric of your wedding day is often made up of joyful pieces from the past, as well as the present. . .

The young woman walked up the attic stairs. Her hand searched the dark wall until she found the light switch, and then she pushed an old wool coat to one side to reach a shelf. Carefully, she lifted a large box from a shelf and blew off a layer of dust. A card was attached by a ribbon to the box, and the young woman sank down on the floor to read it. Leaning against an old trunk, she opened the card.

Dear Daughter,
By the time you read this, I will be gone. These precious
pieces are my wedding gifts to you. May you wear them
with joy. Congratulations!

Love,
Mom

The young woman untied the frayed cord that held the box shut. Gently, she lifted out a Duchess satin wedding gown, then got to her feet and slipped it on. With some tailoring, she decided, it would fit just fine. She reached for the next object in the box: a piece of illusion veiling that covered her hair and draped below her shoulders.

After a few moments of daydreaming, she opened the trunk. The lid creaked as it flipped back on brass hinges. She reached inside and pulled out a white handkerchief. Her fingers rubbed the embroidered blue roses and the tatting along the hems. The young woman tucked the handkerchief up her left sleeve, just like Grandma always had. Another precious piece from the past.

The other treasure in the trunk was a quilt, pieced by her grandmother. The young woman spread it out and smoothed away the wrinkles. Sitting there in the silent attic, the precious fabrics from the past seemed to speak to her. Like the quilt, together the pieces formed a pattern, a pattern she could follow in her marriage.

The satin gown reminded her to pray that smooth stretches of health and prosperity would follow her wedding day. The quilt spoke to her of security, warmth, and comfort, even on the coldest winter nights. Grandma's cotton handkerchief reminded her that she could be simple and pretty at the same time. The illusion veiling revealed to her heart the joy of mysterious, unexpected expressions of love.

Thirty years later, a woman opened an old trunk and chose several pieces of fabric. As she quilted a bridal wall hanging for her daughter, a familiar pattern emerged. She smiled and glanced from the wall hanging she was creating to the old quilt that covered her bed. On an impulse, she embellished the wall hanging with a white handkerchief embroidered with blue roses, a piece of illusion veiling, and Duchess satin ribbons. When she was done, she added her final decoration—cross-stitched words: Precious Pieces of Joy.

DONNA LANGE

My life, my dear sweet life, my life-light, my all,
my goods and chattels, my castles, acres, lawns, and vineyards,
O sun of my life, sun, moon, and stars, heaven and earth, my past
and future, my bride, my girl, my dear friend. . .my heart blood,
my entrails, star of my eyes, O dearest, what shall I call you?

HEINRICH VON KLEIST (1771–1811)

*You learn to speak by speaking,
to study by studying, to run by running,
to work by working; and just so you learn to
love. . .by loving. Begin as a mere apprentice,
and the very power of love will lead you
on to become a master of the art.*

FRANCIS OF SALES (1567–1622)

Something Blue. . .

It rained on my wedding day. The air was so hot and heavy with moisture that my gown felt damp even inside the church. When we left to drive to the reception hall, the sky was filled with towering gray clouds that rumbled and flashed. But as I got out of the car, the clouds suddenly parted for a moment. The sun streamed out in a long golden shaft, and I saw a patch of deep, deep blue beyond the clouds.

You'll find plenty of storms in your married life. But never forget that clouds are just temporary things. Beyond them, if you're patient, you'll find that the sky is just as blue as ever.

Whether or not you make a place in your wedding
for something borrowed and something blue. . .
may you always find in your life the fabrics of joy and peace,
trust and security, and most of all love.
Congratulations!
Welcome to married life!

*The marriage ceremony isn't like graduation;
rather, it's similar to the first day
of kindergarten!
It's not the culmination, but the beginning.*

Susan Alexander Yates